# BASIC

## *Baseball*

## STRATEGY

# AN INTRODUCTION FOR COACHES AND PLAYERS

## S. H. FREEMAN

**McGraw·Hill**

New York   Chicago   San Francisco   Lisbon   London   Madrid   Mexico City
Milan   New Delhi   San Juan   Seoul   Singapore   Sydney   Toronto

The **McGraw·Hill** Companies

**Library of Congress Cataloging-in-Publication Data**

Freeman, S.H. (Serge Herbert), 1925–
    Basic baseball strategy / S.H. "Chuck" Freeman ; photography by Andre Hreha.—Rev. ed.
       p.   cm.
    Includes index.
    ISBN 0-07-145501-9 (alk. paper)
    1. Baseball.   I. Title.

GV867.F76   2006
796.357′2—dc22                          2005030040

1 2 3 4 5 6 7 8 9 0 DOC/DOC 0 9 8 7 6

ISBN 0-07-145501-9

Interior photographs by Andrew Hreha unless otherwise noted

McGraw-Hill books are available at special quantity discounts to use as premiums and sales promotions, or for use in corporate training programs. For more information, please write to the Director of Special Sales, Professional Publishing, McGraw-Hill, Two Penn Plaza, New York, NY 10121-2298. Or contact your local bookstore.

This book is printed on acid-free paper.

# CONTENTS

# FOREWORD

To put first things first, I'd like to make it plain that I believe playing baseball should be fun, especially for the young. For their individual development, as well as for the enjoyment of doing for themselves and by themselves, they should have the minimum of parental playing-field supervision and adult instruction.

It's absolutely essential that boys—and girls, if they're part of the gang or playing softball among themselves—spend their early years learning to swing a bat and catch a ball. The fundamentals (and the fun) must come first.

There is a time, though, when the pride of performance becomes important. That's when the other things come in that are vital to better—and winning—baseball.

Even before my appointment as special consultant to the president, I'd known the value of physical fitness to playing better and longer. Because my father believed in the old-world turnverein [i.e., gymnastics clubs] idea, gymnastics gave me a strong body. And to play superior baseball, it's necessary to develop strength, coordination, and stamina.

Baseball is a game of thinking, too. The physical *and* the mental aspects make for winning. A winning player learns to anticipate plays afield so he'll throw to the correct base if the ball is hit to him. He learns how to execute relay throws and how to hit the cutoff man. And he remembers to hustle and back up his teammates to prevent disaster in case of an overthrow.

A winning player learns to bunt because baseball is a team game. He learns how and when to run the bases, when to be daring and when to be cautious. And he learns how to slide properly, to avoid the tag as well as an injury that could take him out of the lineup.

I played against and for one of the shortest men ever to play in the big leagues—Eddie Stanky. Eddie made himself a winner. He learned to crouch and to foul off pitches so that he could wheedle walks. He became adept at executing the hit-and-run play. He proved that the finer points can mean so much—like hitting the ball to the right side of the infield with none out so that a teammate on second base can take third, where he can score on a fly ball.

Eddie Stanky, who didn't have as much basic talent as many players, played on three pennant-winning teams in three different cities by emphasizing tactics, strategy, and team baseball. Baseball is, as I was saying, a physical and mental game. Playing should be fun. I know winning is.

—*Stan Musial*

# PREFACE

The purpose of this book is to help coaches and managers better understand correct offensive and defensive baseball technique and strategy. It is important for coaches to acknowledge that hitting, throwing, and catching are integral parts of the game, but just part of the whole picture. The proper execution of offensive and defensive situations is vital for the entire coaching picture to evolve.

The strategy and play situations that you are to analyze and understand are exactly the same whether the game is played in Yankee Stadium or in a local ballpark. After viewing some games of the week on national television, it has occurred to me that a copy of *Basic Baseball Strategy* might be an excellent Christmas gift for some big-league managers.

The tips at the end of each chapter are summaries of the important points for you to remember and emphasize. As a college baseball coach I would instruct and drill our players in these same fundamentals. I found myself answering the very same questions your players might be asking. I hope those answers will be here for you.

The supply of professionally trained teachers and coaches was never intended to be directed at the youth sports programs. For more than a half century, parent-coaches have admirably picked up the slack. They have organized, equipped, and maintained amateur baseball teams and ball-

parks. Clinics sponsored by civic groups, recreation depart-
ments, colleges, and professional teams have helped to further hone their knowledge and technique of coaching
baseball. It is my wish that this book might continue to help
lighten your load and make coaching baseball more fun for
you and the players.

# ACKNOWLEDGMENTS

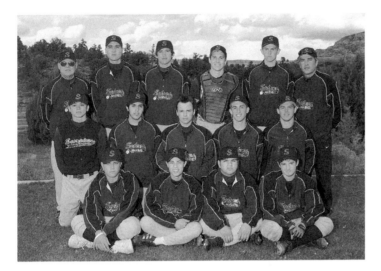

Sedona Red Rock High School baseball team
*(photo by Ron Christopher)*

Thanks are in order for the support of Sedona Red Rock High School principal Russell Snider, athletic director John Parks, and the members of the baseball team. I wish to recognize Andrew Hreha, photographer, who is also a student at SRRHS and who works magic with his digital camera. Best wishes to you in your chosen profession. I would also like to acknowledge the artistic contributions from my wife, Elsie. And, finally, a special thanks to Mark Weinstein, my most patient editor at McGraw-Hill.

# 1
## PART

# OFFENSIVE STRATEGY

Unfortunately, many youth coaches and even professional managers define offensive baseball as simply
batting the ball and running the bases. Well-coached teams
are exposed to the *what*, *when*, *where*, and *why* of every aspect
of the offensive game. For example, *Basic Baseball Strategy*
explains when and why to take a pitch, when and how to

execute a steal or a hit-and-run, and the proper way to lead off and run the bases. It is important that coaches and managers understand the strengths and weaknesses of all their players. However, every team at every level should be able to understand and execute the basics offered in this book.

## CHAPTER 1

# THE TAKE

## WHY WE TAKE A PITCH

The "take" sign tells your batter that he must not swing at the ball regardless of where the pitch might be. The purpose of the take is to make the pitcher work a little harder. If the pitcher is wild and can't get the ball over the plate, it would not be wise for the batter to help him regain his control and confidence by swinging at the first pitch. Another take situation might find your team behind. Base runners are needed. A base runner scoring from a walk is contributing as much as a player who hits a home run. Your team can't score runs without base runners. Taking pitches in certain situations can help players get on base and win games.

# WHEN TO TAKE A PITCH

Four game situations should determine when your batter should take a pitch:

- **The score.** If your team is behind by three or more runs, your batter should not swing at a ball until the pitcher has thrown a strike. It's the "making the pitcher work" strategy. A series of walks can demoralize a team in the field faster than any other play.
- **The hitter.** An exception to this rule would occur if your team has tying or catch-up runs on base with runners at least on second and third. In this situation, if one of your better hitters is at bat, he might be allowed to swing at a "good" pitch.
- **Pitcher's control.** When a pitcher is wild, regardless of the score, it would be wise for your batter to take a pitch.
- **The inning.** Regardless of the inning, when your team is behind, base runners are needed in order to get back in the game. Swinging at the first pitch helps the pitcher. It is even more important in the later innings. The starting pitcher would be getting tired; a relief pitcher might be wild.

There are specific ball and strike situations when your batter should be looking for a take sign: 0-0, 1-0, 2-0, 3-0,

3-1. The take sign should never be given when your batter is behind in the count. Rather than stand perfectly still when taking a pitch, the batter might fake a bunt. This can possibly unnerve the pitcher and cause the infielders to change their positions. However, it is best not to move around too much as it might be a distraction to the umpire.

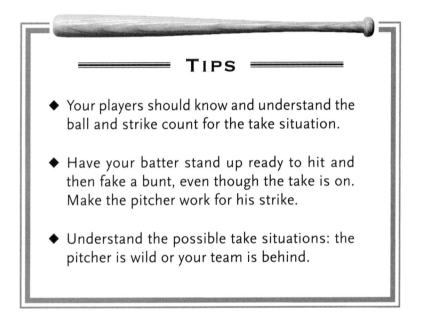

## TIPS

◆ Your players should know and understand the ball and strike count for the take situation.

◆ Have your batter stand up ready to hit and then fake a bunt, even though the take is on. Make the pitcher work for his strike.

◆ Understand the possible take situations: the pitcher is wild or your team is behind.

# 2
CHAPTER

# THE SACRIFICE

## WHY WE SACRIFICE

The sacrifice play is an attempt to bunt the ball down either baseline in order to move a runner or runners into scoring position. We give up an out when we sacrifice; it's for the good of the team. By sacrificing, or bunting, there is less chance of hitting into a double play. A good bunt is difficult to defend against; thus, it becomes a doubly important offensive play. A player with good speed and a solid bunting technique can be an excellent offensive weapon and can "drag bunt" for a base hit without a sign from the coach. When your players attempt to bunt, be sure that they attack only low pitches. The high pitch is easily popped up.

## WHEN TO SACRIFICE

How often the sacrifice is used will be determined by your coaching style and the various strengths of your team. Some coaches play for one run regardless of the team's batting strength. Some coaches play for the "big inning." However, in the late innings of a close game, when one run might mean victory, you shouldn't hesitate to use the sacrifice.

The sacrifice can be used when the score is tied or your team is no more than two runs behind; it is of little value if your team is three or more runs behind. The sacrifice can also be used when your team doesn't have a big lead and you want to add some "insurance" runs. The sacrifice can be used with one out if a weak batter is at the plate; if he were to strike out or hit into a double play, a possible scoring opportunity could be lost. There are three reasons for having your pitcher or weak hitter bunt with one out:

- The chance of a double play is eliminated.
- The chance of your pitcher becoming a base runner is lessened. He can rest in the dugout.
- A runner or runners will be in scoring position with the top of your batting order coming up.

## WHERE TO SACRIFICE

With a runner on first, every attempt should be made to force the first baseman to field the bunt. He must hold the runner on and cannot break for home plate until the pitch is made.

With runners on first and second, the third baseman should be the target of the bunter. By making the third baseman field the bunt, the chance for a force play at third is reduced.

When the pitcher goes to his stretch and both the third and first basemen charge home plate, it is good strategy to have your batter fake a bunt and then swing away. Your batter may not hit the ball, but he plants a seed of doubt in the minds of the corner infielders.

Hitting stance for sacrifice bunt

The base runner has several serious obligations. He must not leave for the next base until he sees the ball bunted on the ground. If he runs when the pitch is made and the ball is popped up, an easy double play can result.

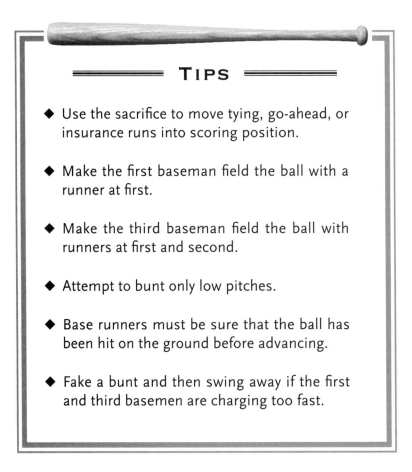

### TIPS

◆ Use the sacrifice to move tying, go-ahead, or insurance runs into scoring position.

◆ Make the first baseman field the ball with a runner at first.

◆ Make the third baseman field the ball with runners at first and second.

◆ Attempt to bunt only low pitches.

◆ Base runners must be sure that the ball has been hit on the ground before advancing.

◆ Fake a bunt and then swing away if the first and third basemen are charging too fast.

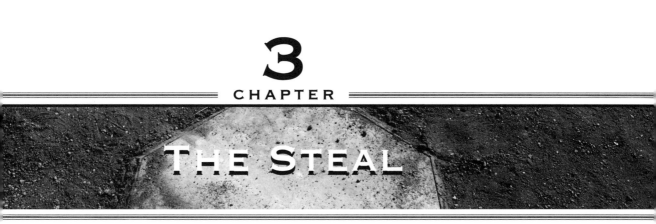

# 3

## CHAPTER

# THE STEAL

### WHY WE STEAL

The steal is a technique used to advance a runner into scoring position. The success of this play usually depends upon two factors: the speed of the runner and his ability to "get a jump" on the pitcher. Of the two, speed is less important than base-running skill. Fast men are not necessarily good base stealers. In fact, historically, some of the better base runners have had only average speed but have had an acute sense of timing. They constantly study the opposing pitchers and catchers.

### WHEN TO STEAL

The steal has no strategic value when your team is more than one run behind. In a close game, the object of the steal

11

is to move a tying, go-ahead, or insurance run into scoring position. Having a runner thrown out when your team is more than two runs behind could possibly take you out of a big inning.

It is important that the batter know when the steal is on and that the steal sign be given when the batter is even or ahead in the count. The batter can swing and miss intentionally, keeping the catcher from coming forward too soon. Some managers allow their good base runners to steal on their own. This can be dangerous, even in the big leagues. As we've discussed, there are specific times to attempt a steal. You should be the only one to make that decision.

## STEALING THIRD BASE

The only logical reason for an attempt to steal third is to put your tying, winning, or insurance run at third with fewer than two outs. If the steal is successful with two outs, your runner still can't score on a sacrifice fly ball. If there is no one out, the runner can score from second on a base hit. Attempt the steal of third only with one out.

## THE DOUBLE STEAL

The double steal with runners on first and second can be used successfully if the defensive team is expecting a sacrifice bunt. As your hitter turns to bunt and the third baseman moves slowly toward home, the runner at second starts for third base. The trailing runner at first must always be alert as to what the runner ahead of him is doing. His actions are always determined by the actions of the advanced runner.

## THE DELAYED DOUBLE STEAL

The delayed double steal, attempted only with runners at first and third, can be an effective and a fun way of getting a run with two out without hitting the ball. It is called the delayed steal because the runner at first does not break for second until the catcher is about to return the ball to the pitcher. If the catcher decides to throw the ball to second base, the runner at third breaks for home as soon as the ball clears the pitcher's head. The runner going from first to second should stop about 20 feet from second base. This maneuver prevents the infielder from tagging the runner. The fielder covering at second must catch and return the ball to home, throwing on the run. If he decides to hold the ball and chase the runner coming from first, he must tag the runner out before the player from third base crosses home plate, or the run counts.

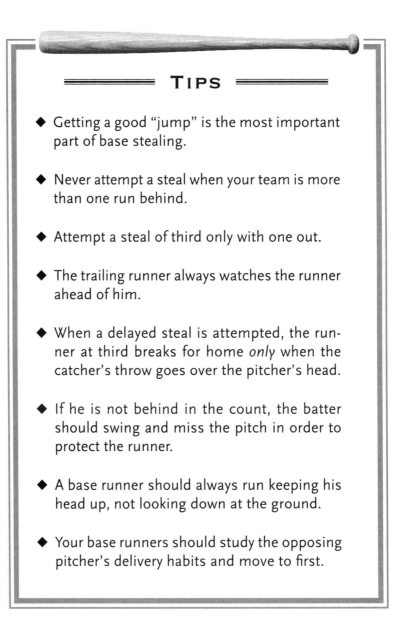

## TIPS

◆ Getting a good "jump" is the most important part of base stealing.

◆ Never attempt a steal when your team is more than one run behind.

◆ Attempt a steal of third only with one out.

◆ The trailing runner always watches the runner ahead of him.

◆ When a delayed steal is attempted, the runner at third breaks for home *only* when the catcher's throw goes over the pitcher's head.

◆ If he is not behind in the count, the batter should swing and miss the pitch in order to protect the runner.

◆ A base runner should always run keeping his head up, not looking down at the ground.

◆ Your base runners should study the opposing pitcher's delivery habits and move to first.

4

# THE HIT-AND-RUN

## WHY WE HIT-AND-RUN

The object of the hit-and-run is to advance a runner a maximum distance with a minimum amount of effort. Your runner who is on first base breaks for second in an attempt to steal. If the batter is right-handed, the second baseman moves to the bag to take the throw from his catcher. Normally, if a left-handed batter is up, the shortstop would take the throw from the catcher. The tricky part of the play involves the batter attempting to bat a ground ball into the spot vacated by the second baseman. Making some kind of contact is vital. The runner would continue on to third.

With the proper talent, many managers would rather hit-and-run than sacrifice. The offensive object is to move as many runners around the base paths to home plate in the fastest method possible. The sacrifice, the steal, and the hit-and-run are attempts to accomplish this objective in a strategic and effective manner.

When your players properly execute the hit-and-run, it has two advantages over the sacrifice. First, an out is not given up in order to advance the runner. Second, your runner moves an extra base, all the way to third. This is one of the few times when a batter might intentionally swing at a bad pitch. The batter must try to hit the ball in order to protect the runner. Even if he misses the pitch, his swing should keep the catcher back long enough for the runner to steal second.

The hit-and-run is one of the more difficult offensive maneuvers, but it is one of the most exciting and colorful to watch. Having your players concentrate on making contact with the ball in batting practice can boost their confidence and increase your team's offensive potential.

## WHEN TO HIT-AND-RUN

You can call for the hit-and-run when ahead, tied, or not more than one run behind. It should be attempted with fewer than two outs, placing a runner at third with the chance of scoring on a fly ball to the outfield. The hit-and-run should be attempted when the batter is ahead in the count: 0-0, 1-0, 2-0, or 3-1. With the second baseman moving toward the bag, the entire right side of the infield is open. Almost any kind of a ground ball to that side will get the job done. In fact, emphasize and remind your players that all they have to do is make contact, as in a pepper game.

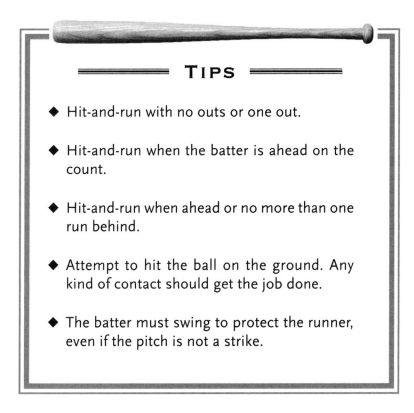

## TIPS

◆ Hit-and-run with no outs or one out.

◆ Hit-and-run when the batter is ahead on the count.

◆ Hit-and-run when ahead or no more than one run behind.

◆ Attempt to hit the ball on the ground. Any kind of contact should get the job done.

◆ The batter must swing to protect the runner, even if the pitch is not a strike.

# 5

# THE SQUEEZE PLAY

## WHEN TO ATTEMPT THE SQUEEZE PLAY

The squeeze play is an attempt to score a runner from third by bunting the ball down either baseline. At best, it is a dangerous and difficult offensive play. It has probably failed as many times as it has been successful. However, if not overdone and if executed by the proper players, it can have a place in your team's offensive strategy. Smart baseball dictates that you use the squeeze play in the following situations:

- There should be fewer than two outs.
- There should be fewer than two strikes on your batter.
- The man at third must be a better-than-average base runner.

- The batter should be a better-than-average bunter.
- The run you are attempting to score would be no less than the go-ahead run.

### THE SAFETY SQUEEZE

The runner at third does not break for home until he sees the ball safely on the ground. Not like a sacrifice, the batter waits until the last second before turning to bunt. In fact, the most effective bunt would be a drag bunt. If the ball is not bunted properly, the runner can remain safely at third.

### THE SUICIDE SQUEEZE

As far as your batter is concerned, there is no margin for error. He must bunt the ball safely on the ground. The runner starts for home as soon as the pitcher begins his windup. Occasionally, a pitcher will stop in the middle of his windup as he sees the runner move toward home. This would be a balk, and the runner would get a free pass to home plate. If your batter doesn't bunt the ball, the runner is a "dead duck" at home.

## WHO IN YOUR LINEUP SHOULD ATTEMPT A SQUEEZE PLAY?

With one or no outs and the go-ahead run at third, it would *not* be a good idea for your third, fourth, or fifth hitters to attempt a squeeze. It's not a hard and fast rule, but your best hitters are expected to hit the ball and drive in runs. It would be more logical for them to drive in a run with a base hit. In theory, the best bunter on your team should be the pitcher. In college and at the professional level (except in the American League), coaches and managers expect their pitchers to practice bunting when taking batting practice.

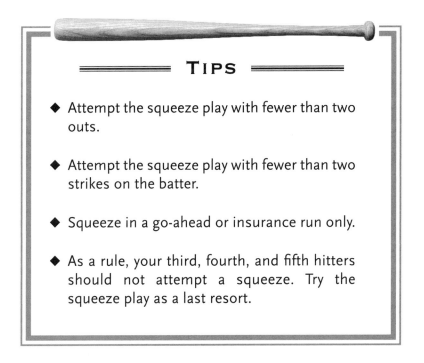

## TIPS

◆ Attempt the squeeze play with fewer than two outs.

◆ Attempt the squeeze play with fewer than two strikes on the batter.

◆ Squeeze in a go-ahead or insurance run only.

◆ As a rule, your third, fourth, and fifth hitters should not attempt a squeeze. Try the squeeze play as a last resort.

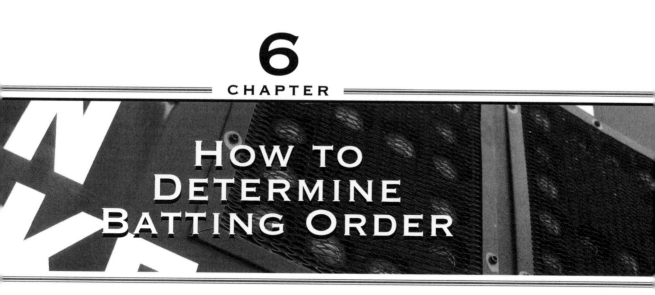

# 6
## CHAPTER

# HOW TO DETERMINE BATTING ORDER

## POSITIONS IN THE LINEUP

In order to set up an offensive strategy, you must decide where each of your players fits most effectively in the batting order. There are four flexible rules of thumb you can observe when making this determination:

- What are the players' running speeds?
- How often do they contact the ball?
- How far do they hit the ball?
- How do they handle a pressure situation?

### YOUR FIRST AND SECOND HITTERS

Your leadoff batter must have patience, have a good eye, and be best at getting on base. A plus would be a left-handed batter who bunts well. The left-handed batter is almost two steps closer to first base. Small size isn't vital, but pitchers have difficulty throwing strikes to short players. Speed is essential. The fastest and shortest player on your team might be a good leadoff man.

The number two hitter should be a good bunter and make consistent contact with the ball, thus being able to utilize the hit-and-run play. He should strike out infrequently. You can teach this hitter to choke up on the bat (move his hands away from the end of the bat) to gain better control.

## YOUR THIRD, FOURTH, AND FIFTH HITTERS

The third, fourth, and fifth batters represent the hitting power of your team. They are the strength of your offense. The two most potent "three-four" combinations in all of baseball history were Babe Ruth and Lou Gehrig of the 1931 New York Yankees, who hit 46 home runs apiece, and Mickey Mantle and Roger Maris, who in 1961 established new power records for the Yankees. No combination of hitters since them has equaled the accomplishments of Mantle and Maris.

Your third hitter could be the best batter on the team. He should have a good batting average, drive in runs, and get on base for your "cleanup" man, the fourth batter. The number four batter's average might be lower than number three, but he should drive in runs with many extra-base hits. If the ability of the third and fourth batters is about the same, then the faster runner could bat third. He's more likely to get into scoring position for number four. Your fifth hitter should be a good RBI man and could interchange with either the third or fourth batter.

### Your Sixth and Seventh Hitters

These players should be able to alternate with the first and second hitters without too much change in your offense. They would be contact hitters, not power hitters.

### Your Eighth and Ninth Hitters

Your team's weakest hitters usually bat eighth and ninth. This doesn't necessarily mean the catcher and the pitcher. It's quite possible that the best player on your team is the pitcher. At the college and professional levels, pitchers tend to concentrate on pitching and don't play every day. At the lower level, if your team has seven power hitters, it isn't suggested that three of them be left out of the lineup. The preceding suggestions apply to the "perfect" situation.

## Platooning the Hitters

"Platooning" means alternating hitters because of an opposing pitcher. For example, some managers will not let a left-handed batter play against a left-handed pitcher. This isn't sound strategy at the lower level, and it's questionable even at the big-league level. Young players should be encouraged to bat against all pitchers. The great hitters in history, from Willie Mays, Ted Williams, and Hank Aaron to current stars Barry Bonds, Manny Ramirez, and Sammy Sosa, have hit all pitchers with equal effectiveness. Your young players should go up to the plate with the feeling that they can hit anyone.

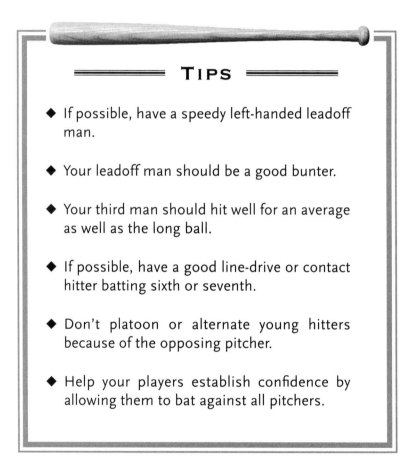

## TIPS

◆ If possible, have a speedy left-handed leadoff man.

◆ Your leadoff man should be a good bunter.

◆ Your third man should hit well for an average as well as the long ball.

◆ If possible, have a good line-drive or contact hitter batting sixth or seventh.

◆ Don't platoon or alternate young hitters because of the opposing pitcher.

◆ Help your players establish confidence by allowing them to bat against all pitchers.

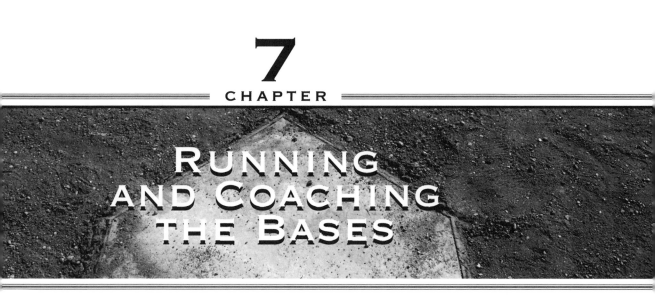

**7**

CHAPTER

# RUNNING AND COACHING THE BASES

## HOW TO RUN THE BASES

Speed can be an added plus to good base running, but it is not the most important factor. These are some basics to teach your base runners:

- The hitter must accelerate from the batter's box as fast as he can. The first 30 feet can be the difference between a base hit or an extra-base hit.
- The batter should not watch the ball.
- On balls hit to center or right field, the batter can determine on his own how big a turn to take at first base. Impress your players with the importance of making a sharp turn, not one halfway into right field.

- On balls hit to the left side of the field, the batter should immediately pick up the first-base coach. He will indicate, "make a turn and hold" or "make a turn and go." If your team has a reputation for running, this can force the defense into committing errors.

## How to Use Your Third-Base Coach

Base coaching can win or lose games. Both your third-base coach and the runner must be aware of the following:

- The score of the game
- The speed and running ability of the player
- The positions of the outfielders

When the runner is some 20 feet from second and is committed to making a turn at second base, he must immediately look for the third-base coach. The third-base coach should signal "stay" or "come."

The distance from second to home is the most difficult to travel. When the runner gets into scoring position, your third-base coach becomes an actor. He will use his arms, body, and voice in an effort to properly advise your runner as he approaches third. There are four possibilities your third-base coach has to offer:

- **Stand up.** The runner should stand up at third if no throw is being made or if he has beaten the throw by a considerable distance.
- **Slide.** When there is the slightest doubt as to whether the runner should slide or stand up, he should *always slide*.
- **Make a turn and stay.** The third-base coach should be 15 to 20 feet down the baseline toward home plate, where he will hold up his hands telling the runner to stay.
- **Make a turn and go.** The coach in the same position down the baseline will vigorously wave the player to home plate.

## HOW TO LEAD OFF

Once your runner has reached base, he should use the same method for leading off and advancing from base to base. Your players (we hope) will have learned in school that the shortest distance between two points is a straight line. When leading off and running to the next base, the runner should go directly from the base, not by way of the outfield.

When leading off third, it is doubly important that your runner stay in the base path with his feet in foul territory and his toes almost touching the foul line. It is important for these reasons:

- It is more difficult for a catcher to determine how far from third your runner is when he is almost on the baseline.
- A batted ball striking a runner in foul territory is a foul ball. If the runner is on the line or in fair territory and is struck by a batted ball, he is out. Once again, have your runners run with their heads up, not looking at the ground.

Batter's correct move to first base

Batter's incorrect move to first base

Correct leadoff position from first base

Incorrect leadoff position from first base

Correct leadoff position from second base

Incorrect leadoff position from second base

Correct leadoff position from third base     Incorrect leadoff position from third base

## COACHING THE BASES

The base coaches are an integral part of your team's offense. How well they do their jobs can determine success or failure. The first-base coach *reminds* more than directs. The batter, properly running to first with his head up, should be able to determine what to do when a ball is hit through to the outfield. Occasionally, when a ground ball goes through an infielder, the first-base coach must vigorously direct the batter to make a turn at first base.

The bulk of the base-coaching responsibility lies with the third-base coach. A good third-base coach can help win games for his team. He must instantly judge whether a runner should slide, stand up at third, make a turn and hold, or, ultimately, continue on to home plate.

Every time your batter walks up to the plate, he's a potential base runner. There is no more important offensive combination than the base coach and the runner. The importance of the base coach is best illustrated by the high salaries they make in the big leagues.

## FIRST BASE

These are the responsibilities of your first-base coach:

- Encourage the runner coming from the batter's box.
- Tell him whether or not to make a turn at first.
- Advise the runner as to the position of the first baseman if he's not holding your runner on.
- Relay signs from the manager.
- Help the runner watch the pitcher's move to first.

## THIRD BASE

The third-base coach must do the following:

- Alert his runner at second as to the movements of the shortstop and second baseman.
- Tell the runner how far to lead off second base.
- Alert the runner of the possibility of a line drive so that he can move back to second base and avert a double play.
- Make sure that a ground ball batted at either third or short goes into the outfield before the runner attempts to advance.
- Tell the runner what to do on a fly ball hit to the outfield.
- Remind the runner of the number of outs.
- Tell the runner to either slide, stand up, or go for home.

The third-base coach must be moving up and down the line depending on what decision is to be made. He must always be well in front of the runner in order to control the runner.

## COACHING AT HOME PLATE

Home plate might be the most neglected area of offensive coaching. The home-plate coach is the "on-deck" batter. It is his responsibility to indicate to the runner whether to slide or stand up. And, if time permits, he should get the bat out of the batter's box.

35

Position of third-base coach when runner must slide

Position of third-base coach when holding runner at the bag

Position of third-base coach when runner turns and holds

Position of third-base coach when runner is waved home

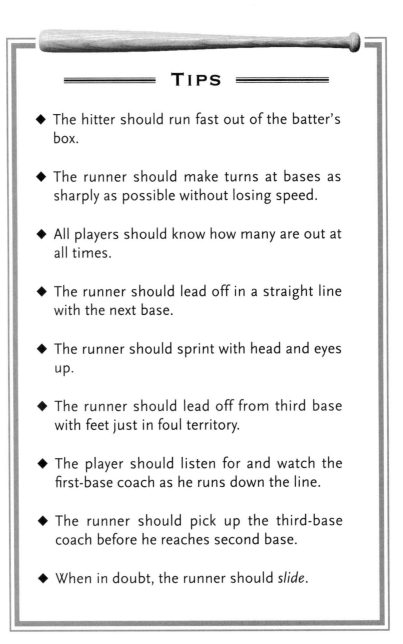

## TIPS

◆ The hitter should run fast out of the batter's box.

◆ The runner should make turns at bases as sharply as possible without losing speed.

◆ All players should know how many are out at all times.

◆ The runner should lead off in a straight line with the next base.

◆ The runner should sprint with head and eyes up.

◆ The runner should lead off from third base with feet just in foul territory.

◆ The player should listen for and watch the first-base coach as he runs down the line.

◆ The runner should pick up the third-base coach before he reaches second base.

◆ When in doubt, the runner should *slide*.

# 8

# THE SIGNS

## WHY SIGNS ARE GIVEN

Once a player leaves the dugout, the only reasonable way to communicate with him is through a series of signs. It should be a simple system, involving only you and your player. There is no need for your base coaches to get involved in sign giving. You shouldn't have to worry about the other team stealing your signs. Most situations are obvious to both sides—the need for a sacrifice bunt or a steal and/or the taking of a pitch. Execution is the key, for both offense and defense.

## HOW SIGNS ARE GIVEN

You can give signs clearly to your players and still keep them simple. For example, your right hand to your nose might be a steal; right hand to your belt could be a hit-and-run; right hand to your ear could be the "take" sign. To make it truly simple, you might give all your signs with your right hand, touching other areas of your body only as a decoy. Use your left hand as another method of confusing the opposition.

## WHEN TO GIVE SIGNS

There is a simple rule to follow to ensure that your players don't miss a sign. Immediately after a pitch has been made, the player, whether he be a batter or a base runner, looks to you for a sign. If this routine is followed, then the only time a sign might be missed is if the player isn't paying attention. Your on-deck hitter will look for a sign as he leaves the batting circle en route to the batter's box. He might look once again just before entering the box.

## HOW THE BATTER RECEIVES A SIGN

Your batter must look at you after every pitch—just a quick peek; he shouldn't stare. A sign won't be necessary after every pitch, but looking creates a good habit. If the batter has any doubt at all about a sign being given, he should ask for a time-out, step out of the batter's box, and quickly look at you. It is also important that your base coaches are aware of the signs in order to assist the base runners.

# SIGNS AND OTHER RESPONSIBILITIES FOR THE BASE RUNNER

The base runner has more to do than run from base to base. For example, let's say your batter has just singled to left field. As he returns to first base after making a turn, he should look over the entire baseball field. He will check the three outfielders to determine their positions and how deep they're playing. That could help him decide how successful he might be in advancing an extra base. Finally, he should quickly look at the third-base coach, the dugout, and the first-base coach. This routine accomplishes several things. First, from a strategic point, the player is aware of defensive positions, he has looked at you for a possible sign, and he checks with his base coaches. Most important, the player is forced to keep his head in the ball game. He won't have time to chitchat with opposing players or look for his girlfriend in the grandstand.

## THE NECESSARY SIGNS

There are five basic signs that will take care of a team's offensive needs. It is possible to get by with fewer than five, but you certainly won't need any more. These basic signs are the take, the sacrifice, the steal, the hit-and-run, and the squeeze. Remember, signs and sign giving should be uncomplicated.

## TIPS

◆ Have specific times for signs to be given.

◆ Keep signs few and simple.

◆ The player should not stare at the coach. Be casual.

◆ Teach your players to think along with you and to understand play situations and their logic.

◆ If a sign is missed, have your player call a time-out and check with you.

# 2
## PART

# DEFENSIVE STRATEGY

## A NOTE ON DEFENSIVE PLAYS

The defensive positions and moves that we are about to discuss should be employed by every team from Little

League to the big leagues. Unfortunately, they are neglected at every level. They are very logical, easy to understand, and simple to execute. It is important that you coach to the level and age of your team; patience is vital. With that in mind, the results will make for a sound defensive baseball team.

Every possible defensive play situation that could develop is accounted for in the following pages. Each player has a basic assignment, and each player's movements will become automatic. Nothing can be more gratifying to a coach, player, or fan than to see a correctly executed defense against a sacrifice, a perfect relay from an outfielder, or the proper cutoff, to name a few.

# 9

# CUTOFF PLAYS

Cutoff plays are essential to make sure that the base runners don't take an extra base on a poorly thrown ball from an outfielder. Your cutoff man, any one of the four infielders, will line up the throw from the outfielder. The cutoff man is the target.

Remember, there is a specific defensive position for every player in every possible play situation. Knowing what to do and where to go for each play will eliminate confusion and will put wins in your team's victory column. Major-league managers place their men in the same positions that you are about to review. Some minor changes can be made depending upon the ability of your team. On a base hit to the outfield with a runner in scoring position, your infielders will take positions in the infield that will enable them to either cut off the outfielder's throw or allow it to go through to a base.

## YOUR CATCHER

The catcher is the key to a successful cutoff play. His judgment will determine whether there should be a play at home plate. He must yell one of three commands:

- "Let it go," anticipating a play at home plate
- "Cut," followed by the base where the ball should be thrown
- "Cut," followed by, "Hold the ball, no play!"

## YOUR THIRD BASEMAN

The third baseman is the cutoff man on balls hit to left field with a runner in scoring position. The first baseman in this situation is thus allowed to remain at first, minimizing the length of the turn taken by the batter rounding first base.

The third baseman moves about 20 feet down the line toward home plate. The shortstop runs to cover third, the second baseman breaks for second, and the pitcher backs up home plate. As the throw comes in from left field, the catcher tells the third baseman what to do with the ball—"let it go" or "cut."

## YOUR FIRST BASEMAN

As soon as the first baseman sees the ball hit to left-center, center, right-center, or right field, he knows that he will be the cutoff man if the ball is thrown to home plate. The third baseman stays at third in case the runner attempts to advance. It is easier for the first baseman to cut off on balls hit from left-center to right. He has a shorter distance to travel from his position at first.

On throws from center and right field, the first baseman will move from a position on the second-base side of the mound almost to the first-base foul line, depending on the accuracy of the throw. On a ball that goes past an outfielder, the batter will continue to second base. The first baseman can still be in cutoff position, in case of an errant throw. There will be no need for him to stay at first.

Cutoff men should attempt to catch every ball thrown by an outfielder unless ordered otherwise by the catcher. The cutoff man should not be standing flat-footed; he should be on his toes, moving toward the ball.

## YOUR SHORTSTOP'S JOB IN CUTOFF SITUATIONS

Besides covering third base when the third baseman is the cutoff man, the shortstop must line up throws from center field to third base and from right field to third base. Lining up a throw means being in the middle and in direct line with the outfielder and his target. On a throw from center field to third base, the shortstop will take a position on the outfield grass about 40 feet from third base. He should be in line

Cutoff positions on base hit to left field (catcher's view)

Cutoff positions on base hit to center and right field (catcher's view)

with the center fielder and third baseman. He can wave his arms to give the outfielder an easier target. He will then react according to the command of the third baseman. When lining up a throw from right field, the shortstop will move toward second base, in line with the right fielder. On all throws to third, the second baseman covers second base.

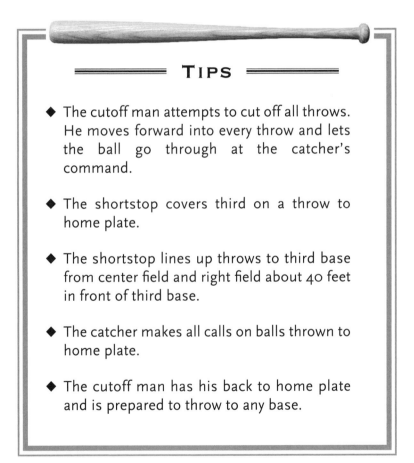

## TIPS

◆ The cutoff man attempts to cut off all throws. He moves forward into every throw and lets the ball go through at the catcher's command.

◆ The shortstop covers third on a throw to home plate.

◆ The shortstop lines up throws to third base from center field and right field about 40 feet in front of third base.

◆ The catcher makes all calls on balls thrown to home plate.

◆ The cutoff man has his back to home plate and is prepared to throw to any base.

# 10
## CHAPTER

# RELAY THROWS

## THE OBJECT OF THE RELAY THROW

Balls are often hit past outfielders and roll to the fence. In most cases it would be impossible for the outfielder to throw the ball all the way to a base with any strength or accuracy. The fastest way to get the ball to the infield is by using your shortstop and second baseman as relay men.

## THE RELAY MEN AND THEIR POSITIONS

• Your relay men take positions about halfway between the point where the outfielder retrieves the ball and the base to which he is throwing. If the ball is fielded at the left-center-field or center-field fence, your shortstop moves to a spot in direct line with second base. On a ball hit to right or right-center field, your second baseman becomes the relay man and the shortstop covers second base. The shortstop and second baseman act as a team directing one another as to where to throw the ball, or to hold it.

- The relay man should never turn his back to the infield as he moves to the relay position. He should shuffle sideways, his right shoulder facing the outfielder and his left shoulder in line with his infield target. In this position, he can turn his head right or left in order to see the outfielder and then the target, making an accurate throw in one motion.

- The relay man should wave his arms and call the outfielder by name. This helps the outfielder to quickly locate the relay man. It is preferable that the relay throw be on one bounce to the intended base. It is easier for the infielder to see and catch a one-bounce overhead throw that bounces about 10 feet in front of the bag. Many low throws in the air can hit a sliding runner.

## THE OUTFIELDER

The success of a relay will depend upon two perfect throws, one by the outfielder and one by the relay man. There are several things an outfielder can do to ensure a perfect relay.

Cutoff man (shortstop or second baseman) receiving throw from outfielder

Relay throw position for either shortstop or second baseman prior to release of the ball

- He must be sure he sees the relay man before he throws the ball. Too many players come up throwing without looking.
- He should throw the ball no lower than waist high and no higher than the relay man's head.
- The ball should be thrown a little ahead of the relay man so that he can catch the ball on the run toward his target, like a forward pass in football.

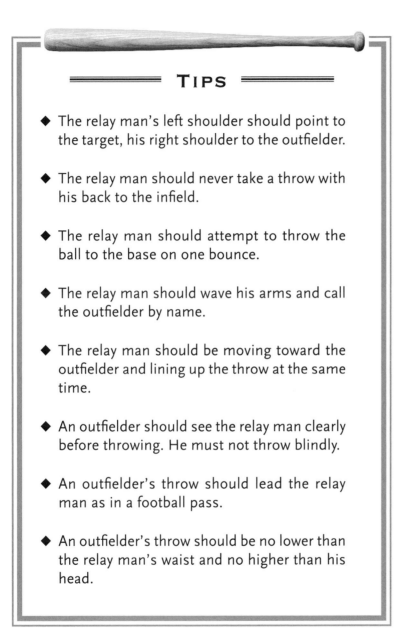

## TIPS

◆ The relay man's left shoulder should point to the target, his right shoulder to the outfielder.

◆ The relay man should never take a throw with his back to the infield.

◆ The relay man should attempt to throw the ball to the base on one bounce.

◆ The relay man should wave his arms and call the outfielder by name.

◆ The relay man should be moving toward the outfielder and lining up the throw at the same time.

◆ An outfielder should see the relay man clearly before throwing. He must not throw blindly.

◆ An outfielder's throw should lead the relay man as in a football pass.

◆ An outfielder's throw should be no lower than the relay man's waist and no higher than his head.

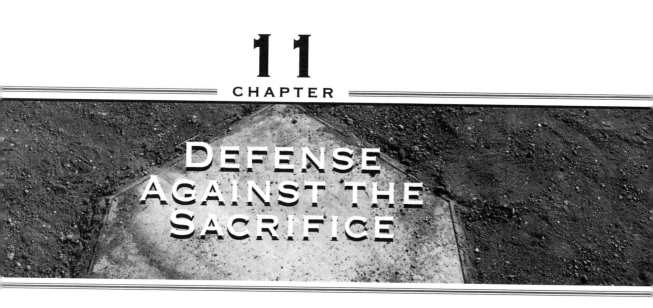

# 11
## CHAPTER

# DEFENSE AGAINST THE SACRIFICE

## INFIELDERS' POSITIONS WITH A RUNNER ON FIRST

- As the pitcher throws to the plate, the third baseman breaks for home.
- The shortstop moves to cover second base.
- The second baseman heads for first.
- The first baseman charges home plate as the pitcher moves off the mound, guarding the third-base side.

A perfect sacrifice bunt will force the third baseman to field the ball close to home plate. This type of bunt should prevent a force out at second. The very second your third baseman realizes that he can't field the ball, he must move quickly back to third. A heads-up runner can take advantage of a lazy third baseman and get an extra base. When the pitcher sees his third baseman field the bunt, he moves quickly to cover third. The catcher must also be aware that he might have to cover third if the pitcher is involved in fielding the bunt.

**Warning!** Even though the game situation might call for a sacrifice bunt, be sure that your infielders are aware of other possibilities—a steal, a delayed steal, or a hit-and-run.

## CALLING THE PLAY

The infielders charging the ball must quickly determine among themselves who will make the play. The fielder who is sure of the ball must call for it. As the ball is fielded, the catcher, with the play developing in front of him, should call the base where the ball is to be thrown.

## INFIELDERS' POSITIONS WITH RUNNERS AT FIRST AND SECOND

With four exceptions, your defense against the sacrifice with men on first and second is the same as with a runner on first.

- With a runner in scoring position, the catcher must stay at home plate.

The third baseman moving toward the bunted ball in a sacrifice situation

The first baseman moving toward the bunted ball in a sacrifice situation

- The first baseman will play off the base and in front of the runner before the pitch.
- It is most important with a runner at second that the third baseman not commit himself to come all the way down the baseline. As the pitcher delivers, the third baseman moves slowly toward the batter until he sees the ball bunted his way. A good fielding pitcher can help his third baseman on this play.
- The shortstop, by faking a move toward second, can help keep the base runner closer to the base. This move by the shortstop might result in a force play at third base. The second baseman must be standing on first base when the ball is bunted. It is difficult for a fielder to throw to a moving target. Again, the second baseman must be moving toward first before the pitcher delivers to the plate.

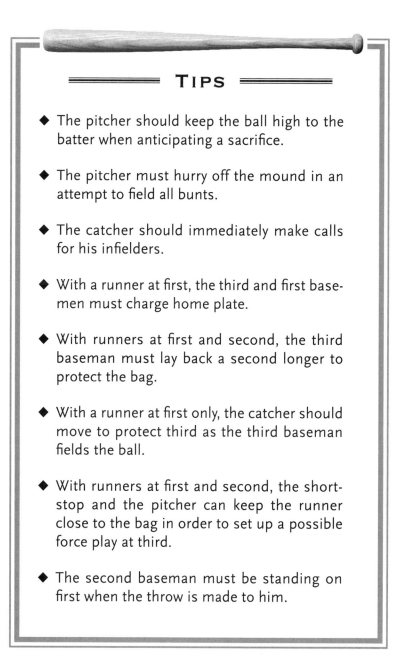

## TIPS

◆ The pitcher should keep the ball high to the batter when anticipating a sacrifice.

◆ The pitcher must hurry off the mound in an attempt to field all bunts.

◆ The catcher should immediately make calls for his infielders.

◆ With a runner at first, the third and first basemen must charge home plate.

◆ With runners at first and second, the third baseman must lay back a second longer to protect the bag.

◆ With a runner at first only, the catcher should move to protect third as the third baseman fields the ball.

◆ With runners at first and second, the shortstop and the pitcher can keep the runner close to the bag in order to set up a possible force play at third.

◆ The second baseman must be standing on first when the throw is made to him.

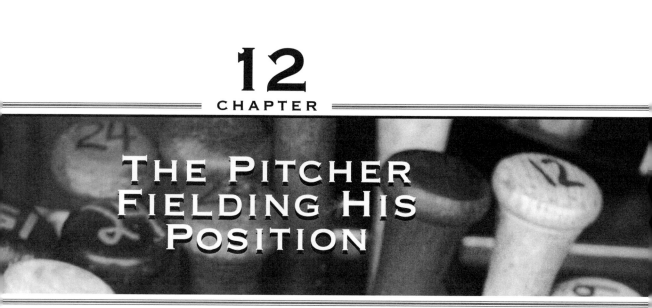

# 12
## CHAPTER

# THE PITCHER FIELDING HIS POSITION

## THE IMPORTANCE OF A GOOD FIELDING PITCHER

Too many pitchers are of the opinion that their only responsibility is throwing the ball to the catcher. Good fielding pitchers strengthen your team and allow the other infielders to comfortably do their job. You can set up fielding drills for your pitchers.

- The pitcher should anticipate ground balls hit to his left, to his right, or directly back to him.
- His first reaction should be to break in the direction of the ball.

- In a sacrifice situation, after his delivery to the plate, the pitcher must be ready to move in any direction to field the bunt.
- If a sacrifice bunt is anticipated, the pitcher should attempt to throw a high pitch to the batter. The high pitch is more difficult to bunt properly and is often popped up.
- The pitcher must respond quickly to directions given by either the first or third baseman.

## BALLS HIT TO THE PITCHER'S RIGHT

The pitcher should be ready to move off the mound in any direction. The most common play for a pitcher is fielding a ball hit to his right. After he's fielded the ball, he must set and throw accurately to first. In most such situations, the third baseman will call the pitcher off the ball and make the play himself.

## BALLS HIT TO THE PITCHER'S LEFT

- On ground balls hit to his left, the pitcher should automatically move toward first base.
- The pitcher's initial line to first should be a few feet to the home-plate side of first base.

Correct line for pitcher covering first base

Incorrect line for pitcher covering first base

- Approximately 10 feet from the bag, the pitcher should be running parallel to the foul line in fair territory. This will eliminate the possibility of a collision with the batter as he approaches first base.
- As the pitcher nears first base, he should slow down in order to be in complete control of his body.
- As the pitcher receives the ball from one of the infielders, he should push off the first-base bag and move into the infield.

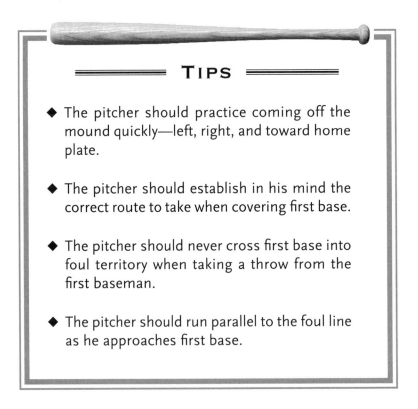

## TIPS

◆ The pitcher should practice coming off the mound quickly—left, right, and toward home plate.

◆ The pitcher should establish in his mind the correct route to take when covering first base.

◆ The pitcher should never cross first base into foul territory when taking a throw from the first baseman.

◆ The pitcher should run parallel to the foul line as he approaches first base.

# 13

# DEFENSE AGAINST THE STEAL, DELAYED STEAL, AND SQUEEZE PLAY

## DEFENSE AGAINST THE STEAL

The vast majority of bases stolen are on the pitcher, not the catcher. If your pitcher does not hold the runner on base properly, your catcher won't be able to throw the runner out on an attempted steal. There are major-league pitchers who have poor mechanics when attempting to hold a runner on base. The opposing teams know and take advantage of this flaw in the pitcher's delivery.

Your pitcher assumes a "stretch" position when about to deliver the ball to home plate with a runner on base. A right-handed pitcher would stand on the mound, his right shoulder facing second base, his left shoulder facing home plate. His right foot would be in contact with the rubber. A left-handed pitcher would be in the opposite position.

Your pitcher must develop moves to first that are deceptive and quick. Being able to vary his moves to first base can be a plus. Many young pitchers allow too much time from the end of their "stretch" position to the delivery of the ball to the plate.

If your pitcher can hold the runner close to the base, the success of the defense against the steal will be determined by four things related to your catcher.

- How well he moves his feet in coordination with his throw
- How quickly he gets rid of the ball
- How accurately he throws the ball
- The strength of his arm

It is a most fortunate team that can boast of a catcher capable of doing all four things well. Realistically, there is no defense against some base runners; Rickey Henderson comes to mind.

# DEFENSE AGAINST THE DELAYED DOUBLE STEAL

In Chapter 3, we talked about the delayed steal as an offensive play. If you have taught your team how it works on offense, you shouldn't have any trouble explaining what to do defensively.

With runners on first and third and the runner breaking for second, your catcher must look at third and throw through to the infielder covering second. Your infielder should take the throw a few feet in front of second base, home-plate side. Once again, it is split-decision time. The key to the defense is the closest infielder yelling, "There he goes," or "tag him." If the runner goes to the plate, he must throw on the run; it is a difficult play at best.

## WHO COVERS SECOND?

When a right-handed batter is up, your second baseman will cover second. When a left-handed batter is up, your short-stop covers when a runner attempts to steal. The rationale for this procedure is that most right-hand batters hit the ball to the left side of the infield. The opposite applies for left-handed hitters. If you know that a certain batter does not hit the ball according to a normal batting pattern, your second baseman and shortstop can adjust accordingly.

Your shortstop and second baseman must talk to each other constantly. They must decide the following:

- Who is going to cover the base?
- Who is going to cut off the throw?
- Who is going to hold the runner close to the bag?
- Who is going to attempt to pick a runner off base?

## DEFENSE AGAINST THE SQUEEZE PLAY

If the squeeze play is expected, your pitcher should throw from the "stretch" position. When the runner on third breaks for home, your pitcher can do one of two things:

- If the runner on third leaves early, the pitcher can take a step back from the rubber and then throw to the catcher. This is now a *thrown* ball, not a pitch—and hence, not a balk. If the batter tries to hit the ball, the umpire can immediately call "interference."
- The pitcher can throw high, under the chin of the batter. This is the most common defense against a squeeze play. The high, inside pitch is difficult to bunt: the batter might pop the ball into the air; or, if he fails to bunt, the catcher can tag out the runner coming from third.

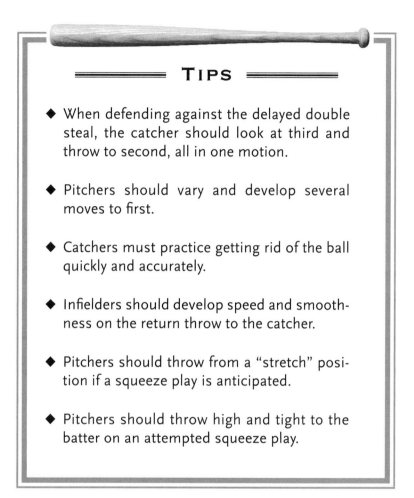

## TIPS

◆ When defending against the delayed double steal, the catcher should look at third and throw to second, all in one motion.

◆ Pitchers should vary and develop several moves to first.

◆ Catchers must practice getting rid of the ball quickly and accurately.

◆ Infielders should develop speed and smoothness on the return throw to the catcher.

◆ Pitchers should throw from a "stretch" position if a squeeze play is anticipated.

◆ Pitchers should throw high and tight to the batter on an attempted squeeze play.

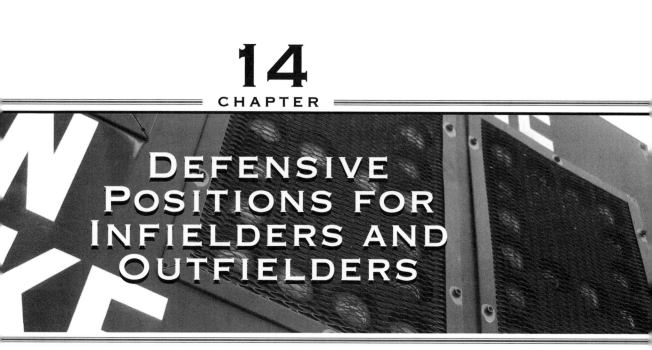

# 14

**CHAPTER**

# DEFENSIVE POSITIONS FOR INFIELDERS AND OUTFIELDERS

## WHY DEFENSIVE POSITIONS CHANGE

As you have no doubt discovered by now, there are many subtle changes that we make both offensively and defensively. The inning, the score, and the caliber of the opposition can determine how your team will set up defensively. How you play it early in the game might change entirely in the later innings. For example, although you might give up a run in the first inning in order to get an out, in the later stages of the game you might instruct your infielders to attempt to throw the runner out.

73

## WHEN TO PLAY THE
## INFIELD BACK

Infielders should play back during the following situations:

- When there is no one on base
- When there is a runner at third, one out or no outs, early in the game, with the score tied or the team in the field ahead

When the infield plays back early in the game with a runner at third, with fewer than two outs, and with your team ahead, you are potentially giving up an unimportant run in order to get an out. In the same situation, if you have your infielders move up, the batter has a better chance of hitting a normally easy ground ball past your infielders. If the run scores, there are still no outs and another runner is on base.

As the coach, you must think, "Our team should be able to score more than one run in the next six or seven innings, so we can afford to give up a run now and get an out." Your infield should always play back when you are two or more runs ahead.

## WHEN TO PLAY THE INFIELD UP

The infield should play up during the following situations:

Infield back—normal position

- With a runner at third, fewer than two outs, and your team one or more runs behind, the infield must play for home plate regardless of the inning.
- Near the end of the game, with the score tied, one or more runs behind, or just one run ahead, it is good strategy for infielders to throw the runner out at the plate.
- With the bases loaded and no one out, your play is to home plate.
- In the same situation, with one out, depending on the strength of your infielders, you might move them back to a double-play position.

Infield up, runner at third, fewer than two outs

# THE DOUBLE-PLAY POSITION
## FOR INFIELDERS

One of the penalties your defense must accept for allowing runners on base is that of giving up ground. For example, when your infielders are all the way back, they have more room to run and field than when they move forward toward home plate. To prepare for a double play, your infielders must move closer to the batter and closer to second base or to the base where they will attempt to start the double play.

- For a double play beginning at second, with a right-handed batter, the third baseman comes forward about two steps.
- The shortstop comes forward about four or five steps and a couple of steps to his left.
- The second baseman moves four steps toward second and five steps toward home.
- If there is a runner only at first, your first baseman stays at the bag and holds the runner on.

The reason your infielders shift a few steps right, left, or back is that they are trying to anticipate where the batter might hit the ball. Most right-handed batters hits the ball to the left side of the diamond; left-handers go to right field.

## POSITIONS FOR OUTFIELDERS

- The position for outfielders can be partially determined by knowing how well each of your opponents hits the ball. Outfielders will play a power hitter deep. They will move toward the foul line if the batter is a pull hitter— that is, hits toward the left-field foul line for a right-handed hitter or the right-field foul line for a left-handed hitter.
- Late in the game, with the tying or go-ahead run in scoring position, outfielders should play a few steps

closer, charge the ball, field it, and throw it in one motion. It is not only a difficult play but a dangerous one as well. But, in the final innings, winning or losing might depend on how well your outfielder can make that play. Obviously, a strong throwing arm is a great positive.

- In the last inning, with fewer than two outs and the winning run at third base, outfielders must play so close that any weakly batted fly ball can be caught and quickly thrown to the plate in order to hold the runner at third. A routine fly ball would easily score the runner.

- On a close play at home, it is imperative that the catcher block the plate, forcing the runner to slide around him. The base runner has the right-of-way and can legally knock the catcher into the grandstand.

- Catchers must perfect their footwork on a force play at home so that they can make an accurate throw to first for a possible double play.

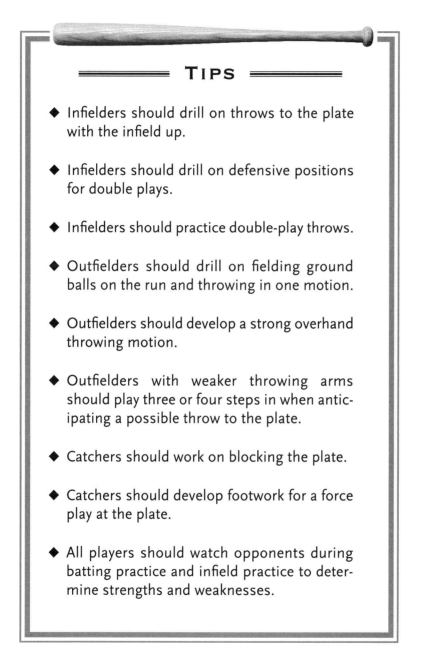

## TIPS

◆ Infielders should drill on throws to the plate with the infield up.

◆ Infielders should drill on defensive positions for double plays.

◆ Infielders should practice double-play throws.

◆ Outfielders should drill on fielding ground balls on the run and throwing in one motion.

◆ Outfielders should develop a strong overhand throwing motion.

◆ Outfielders with weaker throwing arms should play three or four steps in when anticipating a possible throw to the plate.

◆ Catchers should work on blocking the plate.

◆ Catchers should develop footwork for a force play at the plate.

◆ All players should watch opponents during batting practice and infield practice to determine strengths and weaknesses.

# 15
## CHAPTER

# SOME HINTS FOR PITCHERS AND CATCHERS

## PITCHING

### CONTROL

The most important aspect of pitching for young pitchers to learn isn't how fast they throw the ball but *where* they should throw the ball. All the speed in the world won't mean a thing if they can't throw it over the plate. The ideal situation would be for your pitcher to have blazing speed *and* pinpoint control, similar to Randy Johnson, Pedro Martinez, Roger Clemens, and Curt Schilling. These potential Hall of Famers are worth emulating.

Learning to throw strikes should be your pitcher's number one concern in practice. Every chance he gets, he should work on control. Like any other part of the game, control can be learned. Throwing to a catcher would be the ideal situation. If a catcher isn't available, there's always a hanging tire or some poles with string and canvas. In the 1930s the great Dizzy Dean, a farm boy, apparently used inanimate objects as catchers.

The key is a desire to improve.

## TYPES OF PITCHES

Control is sometimes sacrificed in favor of too many different pitches. As a coach, you are obligated to see that your young pitchers throw only two pitches: the fastball and a change off the fastball. When those two pitches are consistently thrown for strikes, your pitchers will win most of their games. Most big-league pitchers throw four pitches, with a few variations: the fastball, the change off the fastball, the curveball, and the change off the curveball. It has been medically established that young pitchers who throw curveballs can cause permanent damage to their arms. Your pitchers should not even think about a curveball until their early teens.

## OUTSMARTING THE BATTER

The real fun begins for your pitchers when they learn to outsmart the batter. This is where changing speeds comes into play. When your pitchers can keep the batters guessing, they'll not only be in control, but they'll win most of their games.

For the older players who can throw a curve, a common mistake they make is throwing a curve every time they are ahead in the count. A good batter can be waiting for that pitch.

Another mistake, made even by professionals, is *not* throwing a curve or off-speed pitch when the pitcher is behind in the count. There's no rule in baseball that states that a pitcher can't throw a curve with the count 3-0, 3-1, or 3-2. Regardless of the type of pitch, your pitcher must have confidence when throwing it, no matter what the situation.

## THE PITCHER AS A FIELDER

A good fielding pitcher will win games. Going a step further, a pitcher who plays good *defense* is an important asset and has these skills:

- He should be able to field ground balls from foul line to foul line.
- He must be able to cover first base when balls are hit to the first baseman.
- He must be able to hold a runner close to the bag and execute a pickoff play.
- He should always be in a proper backup position.

# CATCHING

### THE CATCHER'S DUTIES

The catcher is actually the defensive captain; he's the only player on the field in the best position to view the entire field. Because he can see everything, he is not only in a good position to call the pitches for his pitcher, but he can guide infielders on cutoff plays, back up bases, and set in motion pickoff plays. When there is no one on base, he should move toward first on balls hit to the infielders, backing up first base.

### LEARNING TO WORK WITH THE UMPIRE

Some coaches and players might not agree, but umpires are human. It's vitally important that your catcher establish a good rapport with the umpire. Players who chronically complain about an umpire's calls are hurting their team. As a coach, it is your responsibility to both set a positive example when dealing with umpires and not tolerate any of your players' arguing with or disputing an umpire's decision, regardless of how bad it might be. Remember:

- When your catcher is in the receiving position and wants to say something that is not controversial, be sure he doesn't turn but instead looks straight ahead.

- If your catcher doesn't like a call, he can, in a gentlemanly manner and looking straight ahead, say: "Ump, I believe the pitch was a strike." The ump might say: "You may be right, but I thought it was a little outside." Your catcher can disagree with the umpire as long as he is a gentleman.
- This might seem like fantasyland, but remember, the umpires are friends, neighbors, and volunteers—just like you.
- In all honesty, there are too many of your fellow coaches who are stepping over the line and setting a bad example.

## PICKOFFS

The catcher should have a pickoff sign for each of the four infielders. They should be simple. An example of each could be the following:

- Rub right hand against right thigh—first baseman
- Pick up dirt with right hand—second baseman
- Rub glove along left thigh—third baseman
- Flick dirt with glove—shortstop

Your infielders must have a return sign of their own or else the play is not on. This is a safety measure.

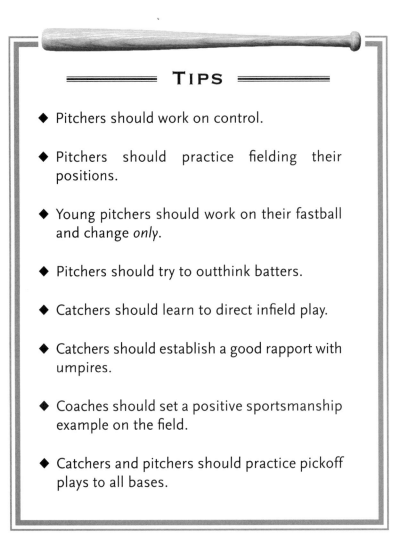

## TIPS

◆ Pitchers should work on control.

◆ Pitchers should practice fielding their positions.

◆ Young pitchers should work on their fastball and change *only*.

◆ Pitchers should try to outthink batters.

◆ Catchers should learn to direct infield play.

◆ Catchers should establish a good rapport with umpires.

◆ Coaches should set a positive sportsmanship example on the field.

◆ Catchers and pitchers should practice pickoff plays to all bases.

# 16
## CHAPTER

# FIELD SIZE, FIELD CONDITIONS, AND WEATHER

## SIZE OF THE FIELD

Modifications of the diamond, or playing area, of the baseball field have been made over the years to accommodate youth baseball programs. The regulation size, 90 feet from base to base and 60 feet, six inches from pitching rubber to home plate, has not changed in a hundred years. However, baseball is the only major sport that doesn't have a regulation-size playing field. The distance from home plate to outfield fences varies from field to field. There is a minimum distance for outfield fences, but no two fields are exactly alike.

## WHERE TO PLAY WHEN THE OUTFIELD FENCE IS CLOSE TO HOME PLATE

- Be sure that your players don't make the mistake of playing with their backs against the outfield fence in a small ballpark.
- If the fences are unusually close to home plate, it would be wise for the outfielders to move closer to the infield in order to catch a ball that would normally fall for a hit.
- Outfielders should still be far enough back so that they could easily run to the fence to catch a fly ball.
- By playing "shallow" or close to the infield, the outfielders can back up the infielders and prevent runners from taking an extra base.

## WHERE TO PLAY WHEN THE OUTFIELD FENCE IS FAR FROM HOME PLATE

In a large ballpark, it is important that the outfielders prevent as many balls as possible from rolling through to the outfield fence. Obviously, some well-hit balls will not be stopped. The outfielder should drop to one knee (right knee for right-handed thrower, left knee for left-handed thrower) on sharply hit ground balls. This maneuver can help prevent ground balls from getting past the outfielder. If a ball gets by an outfielder in a large ballpark, the result might be a three-base hit or an inside-the-park home run.

# FIELD CONDITIONS

Today, most youth ballparks are manicured like big-league fields. But there are still some—fortunately, few—youth baseball fields that are bumpy and in poor condition. On a bumpy field players must be alert; they can't relax on a ground ball for a second. Have your players anticipate a bad bounce on every ball hit to them. That way, they will be ready when it does happen.

## SLOW FIELD

If the grass is high or the field is sandy or damp, the ball won't roll too fast. Infielders should play a few steps closer to the batter. Outfielders can charge ground balls faster. If the ball does get by them, it won't run as fast or as far.

## FAST FIELD

Infielders can play back if the infield is hard and fast. The ball will bounce more sharply and in a lower trajectory. If the infield is hard, then it's logical to assume that the out-field grass or dirt will be equally as fast. Outfielders must guard fast-skipping balls. Backing one another up should be routine.

# WEATHER CONDITIONS

Unlike football, baseball cannot be played if weather conditions become too severe. Baseball should not be played if it is wet or raining; players in the field would slip and slide. The pitcher could not control a wet ball. Runners couldn't run the bases. Also, baseball shouldn't be played in extremely cold weather. Batters couldn't grip the bat, and the fielders' fingers would get too numb to catch the ball. Abner Doubleday, baseball's founding father, was definitely thinking summer for his beloved game.

## WIND

Unless there is a gale blowing, a baseball game can be played on a windy day.

Regardless of the sport, wind is the most undesirable "bad weather" condition. It can affect the normal play of the game and make routine team strategy difficult to achieve. Wind can change the direction of a batted, pitched, or thrown ball.

Defensive players must be aware of the strength of the wind and its direction. For example, if the wind is blowing from left to right field, right-handed batters can be played as if they were left-handed batters. In other words, your defensive outfield must overshift, depending on how hard the wind is blowing.

If the wind is blowing toward home plate, your outfielders should play closer to the infield. The opposite would be true if the wind were blowing out from home plate. Infielders' positions won't change to any degree because they still must field ground balls in the usual manner.

## THE SUN

Learning to play a sunny field is not difficult. If players do not have baseball sunglasses, they must learn to shift their body and to use their glove to shield the sun from their eyes.

Players should learn to play the sun rather than the ball. Teach them to block out the sun, and the ball will be there to catch. For example, if the left fielder is looking into a low, sinking sun, he should move a few steps to the right or left, turning his body a quarter turn toward the batter as he moves. He may be few steps out of position, but he will at least see the ball when it is batted. When the player looks into a sun that is higher in the sky, again, he should turn sideways and shield his eyes with his glove.

# 3

PART

# PHYSICAL AND
# MENTAL PREPARATION

Historically, many baseball teams with excellent talent have not lived up to their potential. Failure is usually a result of little or no mental and physical preparation. Physical mistakes are a part of the game, like booting a ground ball or dropping a fly. Mental mistakes will cost a team more games than poor pitching or fielding. Some of the more serious mental errors are missing a sign, getting picked off base, not hustling on the base paths, throwing to the wrong base, and not hitting the cutoff man. You should set aside a specific period during practice, preferably at the beginning, to work on these fundamentals. Carefully explain to your players the importance of playing "smart" baseball. Players who think on the field are usually winners.

# 17
CHAPTER

# PHYSICAL AND MENTAL MISTAKES

Throwing, catching, and batting a ball are considered the physical aspects of the game. The preceding chapters included the physical acts, such as throwing, fielding, and running. As your players learn to throw and to hit and to pitch, they must also learn and understand another equally important phase of the game: the mental phase. Those of us who have been involved in baseball for many years understand that these are the two aspects of the game that will determine the success of your team. Problems with these are simply referred to as physical and mental errors.

The sad story is that mental errors never make it into a box score, yet they are responsible for far more team losses than are physical errors. A good part of my long and happy coaching career was a result of having been under the influence of my Hall of Fame college coach, Rod Dedeaux at the University of Southern California. Among many other things, he stressed the importance of understanding and eliminating mental errors. Your team can improve by an amazing percentage if your players understand the difference between a physical and a mental error and work to make the corrections.

In terms of classification, there are very few physical errors. Booting a ground ball, dropping a fly ball, and making a bad throw are some good examples. But, mental errors are caused by not thinking ahead, and there are a load of them. Some of the information in the following pages might seem familiar to you. If it is familiar, that is good, because in order to understand mental mistakes, we must sometimes review the strategy that was employed.

## MENTAL ISSUES AT BAT

### MISSING A SIGN

We discussed this earlier, but a little review won't hurt. Your signs should be as few and as simple as possible. How you give them to your players and how they learn to receive them will determine their success. Remember:

- Your batter and base runner should look for a sign immediately after each pitch, preferably when the catcher is returning the ball to the pitcher.

- They should look at you or your coach.
- If a player is not sure of a sign, he should ask the umpire for a time-out and consult with you.
- Your players should learn to anticipate the game situation and be looking for a sign.

## SCORING A RUNNER FROM THIRD WITH ONE OR NO OUTS

One of the most important factors of the game of baseball that you can impart to your players is that of concentrating. It can be a full-time job for many youngsters. Concentration is a vital factor when batting and pitching. Hitting a ball when and where they want to can become a real challenge even for the pros. Be patient with your youngsters. If a player can learn to concentrate, he should be able to get his bat on the ball most of the time. With a runner on third with fewer than two outs, have your players say to themselves, "I'm going to drive in that run." Incorporate a batting-practice drill where they try to hit fly balls and line drives.

## FAILING TO SACRIFICE

Turning around or squaring away to meet the ball should be a simple maneuver for your players. Yet games are lost every day because a sacrifice bunt isn't laid down in an important situation. It is amazing how many multimillionaire major-league players have difficulty laying down a simple bunt.

The only cure for poor bunting is instruction, practice, and concentration.

## COACHING AT HOME PLATE

Your on-deck batter must be ready to tell your base runner, heading for home, what to do. Games have been lost because the on-deck hitter at home was not in position to signal the runner to slide or stand up. His job is even more important than those of the other base coaches because the run scores or does not score depending upon his judgment. The on-deck batter should not be at the bat rack picking out a bat when a runner is coming home.

# MENTAL ISSUES ON THE BASE PATHS

## MISSING THE BASE

When we compare the number of times the bases are stepped on to misses, base missing doesn't appear to be too high up on the list of mental mistakes. But as in the case of most mental errors, missing a base can result in the loss of a game. The runner should not slow up or adjust his step in order to find the base. In other words, he shouldn't break stride in order to step on the base with a particular foot. Each player can develop his own stride so that he can consistently step on the same part of the bag.

## FAILING TO TAG UP ON A FLY BALL

With fewer than two outs, the runner should always tag up at third base on a fly ball to the outfield. There is no "halfway down the line" situation at third base. On a long fly ball, the runner should tag up and score. On a short fly ball to the outfield, the runner should tag up and break for home in order to draw a throw. He would normally stop about 10 feet down the line if the throw continues to the plate.

If the runner is at second with no outs, he can tag up on a ball hit to deep center or right field. A good base runner at first, with no one out, can tag up on a long ball hit to left, left-center, or center. There is no guesswork here. If the runner decides to move to second, he must not be thrown out. With fewer than two outs, on a medium fly ball hit to any place but right field, the runner could go halfway to second. If the ball is caught, he has plenty of time to return to first.

## DOUBLE PLAY ON A FLY BALL OR LINE DRIVE

Being doubled up or doubled off means that the runner wasn't able to get back to the base fast enough after a fly ball was caught. The result is a double play. "Leaving too soon" is the most common and inexcusable base-running mistake. If the runner knows the number of outs and watches the flight of the ball, he should never get doubled up. However, there are two situations when the runner might be doubled off and it wouldn't be his fault. If the hit-and-run play is on and the batter hits a line drive to an infielder, it would be difficult for the runner to return safely to the base. A line drive to the left of the first baseman that is caught might result in a blame-free double play, as the first baseman steps on the bag. One of the admonitions both base coaches should shout at their runners before every pitch is, "Watch out for the line drive."

## GETTING PICKED OFF BASE

The success of a pickoff play depends upon the quickness and cleverness of the defense and the carelessness of the runner and the base coach. If the runner takes a big lead and leans toward the next base, he might get picked off. When most of the runner's weight is on his lead foot, it is difficult to recover in time and slide under a good throw. His weight must be evenly distributed on both feet.

## FAILING TO SLIDE

It's an old baseball axiom: "When in doubt, slide." If the runner hasn't made up his mind to slide long before he gets to the base, he can severely injure himself. Running bases and sliding is fun. I have never been, and shall never be, a fan of the "head-first" slide. It can be dangerous and is a slower method of getting to the base. A fadeaway hook slide or a bent-leg stand-up slide will allow the runner more maneuverability around the base. As with any other base-ball skill, sliding must be taught. When a player learns to do it well, sliding becomes as much a part of his play as swing-ing a bat.

## MENTAL ISSUES IN THE FIELD

### A POOR THROW BY A FIELDER

The single most important part of the defensive game is throwing. Throwing errors directly result in more lost games than all the other defensive mistakes combined. Although your player's throwing of a baseball is physical, his control of where the ball goes is mental. When you teach your players to think about throwing the ball accurately, you will find that they will make fewer throwing errors. If you explain the difference between the pitcher's strike zone and the infielder's throw to the first baseman, they will understand why there is no excuse for a bad throw to first base. The pitcher throws to an area 17 inches wide and about three and a half feet high. If infielders are throwing to a six-foot-tall first baseman, their target is about nine feet high by fif-teen feet wide.

### THROWING TO THE WRONG BASE

Throwing to the wrong base can be eliminated if the player thinks about what to do with ball ahead of time. He must decide where he will throw the ball before it is hit to him. He should review in his mind the game situation before each pitch (i.e., the number of outs, the score, the inning, the strength of the batter, and the position of the base runners).

## MAKING UNNECESSARY THROWS

When a player has no possible chance for a play, he should not attempt to throw the ball. Chances for error increase every time the ball is thrown. His teammates can help. For example, if he juggles the ball, the player nearest to him can yell, "No play! No play!"

## FAILING TO BACK UP A PLAY

It should be an automatic reaction. Every time a ball is batted to one of the players, his closest teammate should immediately move to a backup position.

## PITCHERS COVERING A BASE

Every time a ball is hit to the first baseman, the pitcher sprints to cover first to take a possible throw from him. You must emphasize the fact that the pitcher is the ninth fielder. A good fielding pitcher will help his team and himself win games. To take it a step further, he moves toward first on any ball hit to his left, whether it is a bunt or a home run into the parking lot.

## CALLING FOR A BALL

No fly ball that can be reached should ever be dropped, be it a pop fly to the catcher or a drive between outfielders. Someone must call loud and clear for balls hit in the air. Outfielders coming in should call infielders off of balls they can reach. It is easier for an outfielder to catch a ball in front of him than for an infielder to make a catch over his shoulder with his back to the infield. The shortstop should call for pop flies in back of third. He has a better angle on the ball than the third baseman backpedaling. The second baseman will extend the same courtesy to his first baseman.

## PASSED BALL

A passed ball by the catcher is usually a result of one of two things: crossed signals between the pitcher and his catcher or laziness on the part of the catcher. The term *passed ball* indicates that the catcher should have caught or stopped the ball. The catcher is charged with an error. A *wild pitch*, on the other hand, is the responsibility of the pitcher, a pitch the catcher had no chance of catching. Catchers should be taught to go down on both knees in an attempt to block pitches in the dirt and keep the ball in front of them.

## BASE ON BALLS WITH A GOOD LEAD

Nothing is more frustrating for coaches, players, or fans than a pitcher who can't get the ball over the plate. Another wise baseball saying is: "There's no defense against a base on balls." Four runs would be considered a good lead in a game. A pitcher who gives up a walk with that kind of a lead is not concentrating, he's not pitching—he's *throwing*. Sadly, some of the worst offenders today are major-league pitchers. We had a fine system when I was a college ballplayer; the pitcher had to pay a fee for every walk. It would range from a nickel to a quarter or more. A pitcher's walk with a four-run lead would cost him fifty cents.

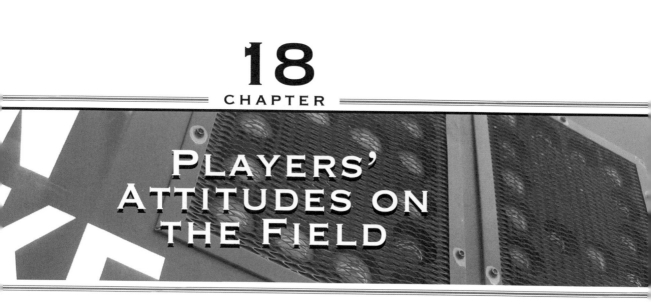

# 18
## CHAPTER

# PLAYERS' ATTITUDES ON THE FIELD

If you were to ask me what I thought was the most important chapter in *Basic Baseball Strategy*, I would have to say Chapter 18. Winning has become an American obsession at every level of competition whether it be the Little League World Series or the National Spelling Bee. The pros go through their prime-time rituals because big bucks are at stake. At the amateur level, the stakes are much higher: integrity, self-respect, and sportsmanship. It all boils down to one thing: we adults must set an example.

## ARGUING WITH UMPIRES

Traditionally, baseball is the only sport where an official's judgment can be questioned without any serious consequences. At the professional level it is considered "part of the game." It is part of the game as long as the right people are involved. Even pro umpires will draw the line. Here, example setting should be the dominant theme for you and your coaches. There are several things you should understand when we discuss umpires:

- Who should be involved in discussions with umpires?
- How long should the discussion last?
- Of what value are the discussions?

First of all, under no circumstances should a young player in amateur baseball (Little League through college) ever debate an umpire's decision. It is understandable that, at every level, the first reaction for a player is to question the umpire's call.

It is your job as the coach to discuss with the umpires any problem that might develop during the course of the game. As the coach, you have the right to express your opinion about a certain play as long as you do so in a gentlemanly manner. A player, team, or coach who continues to argue or yell at an umpire is guilty of extremely poor sportsmanship. Umpires of youth games are usually volunteers and neighbors, and there's little reward for umpiring a youth baseball game. Unfortunately, there is little that can be done about unruly fans. Some "gutsy" umpires have been known to forfeit a game because of unruly fans.

Explain to your team how silly the umpire would look if he yelled at a player every time one of them made a mistake. An umpire makes far fewer mistakes during a game than does a player. If a *rule* is disputed, then you can ask that the game be played "under protest," without arguing with the umpire. Your league president can make a judgment. You may not like an umpire's ruling or decision, but it must be respected and accepted.

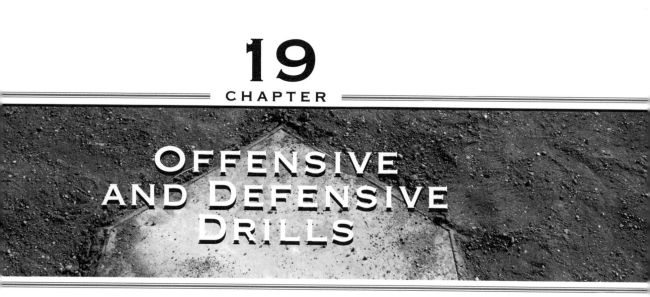

# 19

CHAPTER

# OFFENSIVE AND DEFENSIVE DRILLS

How many times, when watching a professional game, have you, one of your friends, or your kid commented, "Boy, that was a stupid play"? More than likely, the reference was made about a *mental mistake*. We usually have great empathy for a player who boots a ground ball or drops a fly. But, if a pitcher doesn't attempt to cover first in a ball hit to the first baseman, or an outfielder doesn't back up a teammate, or a base runner misses a sign, the comment is, "what a stupid play," and rightfully so.

However, it is almost impossible to separate the physical acts of baseball—running, throwing, fielding, and batting—from the mental part of the game. For example, running down the baseline is physical, but how your players run down the line, how they make the turn at first, and how they use their base coaches all require thought on their part. The team you've worked with so diligently—explaining the mental and physical aspects of the game—will shortly become 15 happy young warriors, making their coach proud.

I would like to leave you with some excellent practice drills. When they are worked on faithfully, they are guaranteed to strengthen the mental and physical phases of your team's game. Practice these drills as if your team were playing a real game.

## OFFENSIVE DRILLS

### DRILL 1: COMBINATION SACRIFICE, HIT-AND-RUN, AND STEAL

#### THE PURPOSE OF THE DRILL

- To practice and perfect the proper techniques of the sacrifice, the hit-and-run play, and base stealing

**HOW TO SET UP THE DRILL.** Use your regular batting-practice routine. Two pitchers can alternate throwing batting practice. A group of five players can be ready to bat. Have your infielders and outfielders take defensive positions.

#### HOW TO EXECUTE THE DRILL

1. The last two men in the group can be base runners at first. The batter should attempt a sacrifice bunt down

each baseline. One runner at first should advance to second when he sees the ball batted on the ground.

2. The first runner remains at second, and the next runner takes his place at first base.

3. The batter attempts another sacrifice with runners at first and second.

4. During the drill, your infielders practice their defensive moves against the sacrifice. This drill allows your pitcher to work with men on base and practice fielding his position.

5. Next, the batter attempts a hit-and-run play with each of his base runners. He tries to make contact with the ball with every pitch thrown to him as the runner on first breaks for second.

6. The final phase of the drill, and an extremely important one, has the batter taking four more swings, *at strikes only.*

Every time a runner leads off from first, whether it be for a hit-and-run or a sacrifice, he should be thinking "steal situation."

Specify batting groups. For example: group one, starting infielders; group two, starting outfielders and catcher; group three, everyone else, except pitchers. Pitchers can take batting practice for 10 minutes before the rest of the team.

You should specify a certain number of swings and a certain number of rounds per group, possibly three rounds of five swings. This tends to make the batter concentrate more on swinging at good pitches, knowing that he gets only five precious swings. After the fifth swing, the batter should sprint to first base. He can then practice stealing second when the next batter comes up to the plate. By the time the runner gets around to third, he can trot back to home plate, ready to bat his second round.

## DRILL 2: BASE-RUNNING AND BASE-COACHING DRILL

### THE PURPOSE OF THE DRILL

- To practice the correct fundamentals of baserunning
- To prepare each of your players so that he may expertly coach first and third base. A technique that worked well for me was to designate nonregular players to the job of coaching first and third base. They not only became proficient at an important position, but they also became an integral part of the game.

**HOW TO SET UP THE DRILL.** Assign players to the first- and third-base coaching boxes. Have the remainder of the squad form a single line at home plate.

### HOW TO EXECUTE THE DRILL

1. The players at the plate pretend to bat the ball and run from home to first. The second player can run when the first player is halfway to first base. The first-

base coach yells at the batter and uses his arms, telling the batter to "stay," "make a turn," or "go."

2. The runners now line up at first base. They will practice leading off and then breaking for second. As discussed before, the runner will look for his third-base coach well before he gets to second. The third-base coach will either wave him on or hold him up.

3. Next, the players will line up at second and repeat the drill, this time heading for home plate.

## DRILL 3: SCORING A RUNNER FROM THIRD AND THE SQUEEZE PLAY DRILL

### THE PURPOSE OF THE DRILL

- To learn to concentrate as a batter
- To have your players improve their bunting skills in relation to the squeeze play

**HOW TO SET UP THE DRILL.** You can utilize your batting-practice procedure, starting with four players at the batting cage. A fifth man can be a runner at third base. There should be players at all defensive infield positions.

### HOW TO EXECUTE THE DRILL

1. The pitcher will say, "no one out and a runner at third base." He will then pitch to the batter as if it were a game. The batter then attempts to get a hit or a run-scoring fly ball. When he scores the runner, makes an

out, or walks, the next batter attempts to do the same thing. It is an excellent concentration drill for both the batter and the pitcher.

2. The five offensive players get together and make up a sign for their own squeeze play. Any time during the batter's turn at bat, he and the runner at third may attempt a squeeze play.

# DEFENSIVE DRILLS

### DRILL 4: RELAY THROWS

#### THE PURPOSE OF THE DRILL

- To ensure strong, accurate relay throws
- To help make your players conscious of the importance of throwing the ball accurately

**HOW TO SET UP THE DRILL.** The drill should include all members of the team except pitchers. Divide your squad into groups of three. Have the members of each group station themselves about a hundred feet apart, closer or farther, depending on their strength and age. If possible, have an outfielder at either end of the line with an infielder in the middle.

#### HOW TO EXECUTE THE DRILL

1. An end player throws the ball to the player in the middle.

2. Next, the middle man throws the ball to the other end man, who acts as the catcher at the end of the relay.

3. Repeat the drill, with the three changing positions. This is an early-season drill that is excellent for improving footwork and body position.

As the season progresses, a "game situation" drill can improve players' skills. Your team takes their normal defensive positions. The pitchers act as base runners. Then, you bat the ball over their heads or between the outfielders, and everyone reacts as if it were a real game.

## DRILL 5: CUTOFFS, DEFENSE AGAINST A DELAYED STEAL, AND RUNDOWN DRILLS

### THE PURPOSE OF THE DRILL
- To familiarize all players with the proper cutoff positions
- To improve the accuracy and speed of the players in the cutoff play

**HOW TO SET UP THE DRILL.** Your team will take their regular defensive positions. Pitchers can be base runners. All of the combinations involving your cutoff men can be practiced, along with a runner in scoring position and the ball hit to left-center, center, and right-center field.

Relay drill

### HOW TO EXECUTE THE DRILL

1. Station your players according to the particular cut-off play to be practiced. Then hit the ball to the outfield, and have players attempt to throw the ball to the correct base. The closest player to the infielder receiving the ball will yell out either the proper base the ball is to be thrown to or "cut, no play."

2. Infielders assume their defensive positions with runners at first and third. The pitcher throws to the batter from the stretch position. The runner at first can attempt a regular steal or a delayed steal, depending upon a prearranged signal with the coach and runner at third. As the runner breaks for second, all of the defensive infielders yell, "There he goes."

3. The catcher can practice throwing through to second, or he can fake a throw to second and then throw to

third. If the runner at third is caught leaning toward home, the infielders can practice the "rundown," or "pickle," play. If the catcher throws through to second, the shortstop can work on his return throw to the catcher.

## DRILL 6: DEFENSE AGAINST A SACRIFICE, PITCHERS COVERING FIRST, AND PITCHERS FIELDING THEIR POSITIONS

### THE PURPOSE OF THE DRILL

- To teach players to react quickly and smoothly to the various situations that occur in the infield

**HOW TO SET UP THE DRILL.** This is a fast-moving drill involving the entire team. Have your infielders take their normal defensive positions. Pitchers form a single line to the third-base side of the mound. Outfielders act as base runners and line up at home plate. As each pitcher completes his part of the drill, he takes his place as a base runner.

### HOW TO EXECUTE THE DRILL

1. The first pitcher in line winds up and throws the ball to the catcher. As the catcher receives the ball, you hit a ground ball to the first baseman. Because there is no runner on first, the first baseman plays away from the bag.
2. The runner at home starts toward first with the crack of the bat. The pitcher sprints off the mound to cover

first and take an underhand throw from the first baseman.

3. The runner remains at first, and the first baseman holds him on. The infield plays for a sacrifice. The next pitcher in line assumes a stretch position and then pitches to the plate.

4. As the catcher receives the ball, you bunt down either baseline or toward the pitcher. The catcher indicates which base the pitcher is to throw the ball to. Your pretend batters should be going from home to first on every pitch.

A new pitcher moves into position on the mound after every pitch. Alternating this way, every pitcher should cover first and field a bunt at least twice.

The photos show the correct sequence of moves for a pitcher covering first on a ground ball hit to the right side.

Pitcher covers first—a sequence of moves

# 20
## CHAPTER

# A TOUR OF THE BASES

You might question why "A Tour of the Bases" is the last chapter of the book. It would seem logical that this chapter would be a good introduction to *Basic Baseball Strategy*, but I've intentionally placed it last to remind you that it should be the *first* information you give out as you and your team leave the dugout after your introductory remarks. I've found it to be a great motivating tool for young players whose interest usually centers on the offensive part of the game.

Taking your team on a "tour of the bases" prior to the season, and reviewing it during the season, can be a most effective method for improving offensive techniques. The "tour" *visually* instructs in methods that were *verbally* discussed earlier. This chapter deals with receiving signs, running the bases, and coaching the bases and will help players learn to understand and anticipate offensive maneuvers and strategy. It begins from the time they leave the dugout until they have crossed home plate.

# FROM THE DUGOUT TO THE BATTER'S BOX

1. The hitter should discuss play possibilities with the coach before leaving the dugout.
2. The on-deck hitter should look for the sign from the coach on the way to the batter's box.
3. The on-deck hitter should remove the bat from batter's box and coach home plate for the runner.
4. The hitter should take one more look at the coach before stepping into the batter's box.
5. The hitter should look for a sign immediately after each pitch.
6. Signs must be given and taken at the same designated time.
7. The batter should not stare at the coach when receiving a sign. If the player is not sure of the sign, he should ask the umpire for time-out and then look again. He can kick dirt from his spikes, pick up a resin bag, etc. If he's still not sure, he should ask the base coach.
8. Players should not *think* a sign has been given—they must *know*.

# RUNNING TO FIRST

1. The batter must run hard from home plate. Extra-base hits are created in the first 20 feet from home plate.

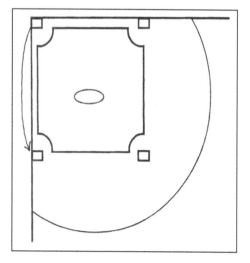

Running to first, making a turn, looking for a sign

2. The runner should run in foul territory from home to first, next to the baseline.

3. The runner should make a big, sharp turn at first when the ball is hit through the infield, at least 20 feet. He should not run into right field; the object is second base.

   • This causes outfielders to hurry and puts the runner in position to take an extra base if the ball is bobbled by an outfielder.

   • The runner should watch the ball when he is returning to first. He must not turn his back toward the ball.

4. On return to first, after a base hit, the runner should scan the field.

123

- The runner should stand on first base, check the first-base coach, outfielders, the third-base coach, and the dugouts.
- He should look for signs after every pitch, just as the batter does.

## MOVING FROM FIRST TO SECOND

1. The runner on first base should lead off slowly and deliberately and then run in the baseline.
2. The runner should have his weight evenly distributed on the balls of his feet.
3. He should not lean toward second base.
4. The runner should watch the pitcher's feet.
5. After leading off, the runner can go back to the bag in two ways:
   - On his stomach
   - Standing up, touching the upper left side of first base with his left foot, and then swinging his body around to face second base
6. The runner should use a crossover step when stealing. A slow-moving lead is preferable to "dancing."
7. On a line drive, the runner's first move should be back to the bag to prevent a double play.
8. When advancing from first to second on a base hit, the runner should look for the third-base coach about 20 feet from second base.

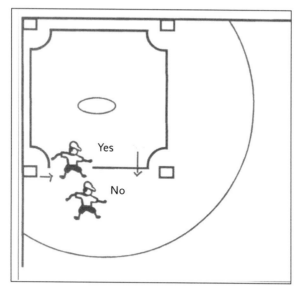

How to lead off, run to second, and steal a base

- When the ball is hit to left or center field, the play is in front of the runner.
- He must know the game situation, score, and number of outs before trying for an extra base.

## LEAVING SECOND BASE

1. The runner should lead off second base exactly as he led off first.
2. The runner should stay in the baseline.
3. The runner should not back up toward third.

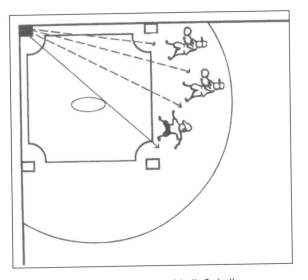

Leading off second base—ground ball, fly ball

4. The third-base coach has a view of the shortstop and the second baseman.
5. If a ground ball is hit in front of the runner, his first move should be back to second.
6. If a ground ball is hit to third base with two out, the runner should hold until the third baseman throws to first.
7. With a line drive and fewer than two outs, the runner's first move should be back to second.
8. If a deep fly ball is hit to right field or right-center with no outs, the runner should tag up.
9. The runner should be halfway down the baseline on all other outfield fly balls.

# THIRD BASE

1. The third-base coach should pick up the runner before he gets to second base.
   - The third-base coach should constantly talk to the runner and direct him with hand signals.
   - The third-base coach should move down the base-line toward home plate before the runner gets to third.
2. On any line drive or ball hit in the air with fewer than two outs, the runner's first move should be back to third.

Coaching third with a runner at second

3. On a "tag-up" situation, the runner should observe the catch and then must decide on his own whether to advance to the plate.

4. The runner should lead off third the same as he would at first and second.

   • Faking and sprinting down the line won't distract most pitchers, and the runner might get picked off.

   • The runner should be in foul territory with his toes up to, but not touching, the foul line. The closer the runner is to the foul line, the more difficult it is for the catcher to determine the length of the lead from third base.

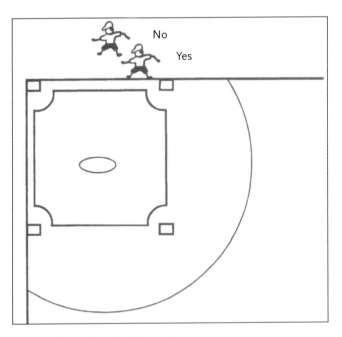

Running from third, leadoff position

5. If the infield is up with fewer than two outs and a runner at third or runners at second and third, the runners must wait to see if the ball is batted through the infield before advancing.

6. On an infield grounder with runners at first and third and fewer than two outs, the runner at third should break for home in order to prevent a double play. If the play is made for him at the plate, he should stop about 10 feet from home and get in a pickle play. This allows runners to move up a base.

# THE LAST WORD

It is important to understand that practice and repetition will be effective when the techniques employed are correct. This philosophy is not in conflict with a player's individual mannerisms. As long as his unorthodox approach does not interfere with his ability to perform properly, no attempt should be made to "make him look good." If we tried to change a .350 hitter's peculiar stance, we might end up with a good-looking .250 hitter.

*Basic Baseball Strategy* deals with offensive and defensive techniques that have been an integral part of the game since it came on the American scene. I hope this book has provided you with the necessary information that might help to improve the skills of your young players. It is fascinating, and makes the game of baseball more enjoyable, when we understand that the game has thrived for more than 125 years with very few changes. With all due respect to football and basketball fans and players, baseball is still America's game.

# INDEX